LEADERS OF
ANCIENT EGYPT

AHMOSE   Liberator
of Egypt

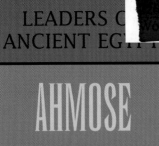

LEADERS OF
ANCIENT EGYPT

AHMOSE

Liberator of Egypt

Susanna Thomas

For George Brown

Published in 2003 by The Rosen Publishing Group, Inc.
29 East 21st Street, New York, NY 10010

Library of Congress Cataloging-in-Publication Data

Thomas, Susanna.
Ahmose: liberator of Egypt / Susanna Thomas.— 1st ed.
    p. cm. — (Leaders of ancient Egypt)
Includes bibliographical references and index.
ISBN 0-8239-3599-X (library binding)
1. Ahmose I, King of Egypt. 2. Egypt—History—To 332 BC.
3. Pharaohs—Biography.
I. Title. II. Series.
DT85.A36 T47 2001
932'.014'092—dc21

                                                        2002001031

Manufactured in the United States of America

CONTENTS

ANCIENT EGYPT

CANAAN

MEDITERRANEAN SEA

• Alexandria

Nile Delta

• Avaris

LIBYA

LOWER
EGYPT

• Heliopolis

• Cairo

Giza •

Memphis •
Saqqara •

Dashur •

Meidum •

FAIYUM

• el-Amarna

SINAI

UPPER
EGYPT

EASTERN DESERT

WESTERN DESERT

Abydos •

• Dendera

• Thebes

• Karnak
• Luxor

River Nile

• Elephantine
• Aswan

RED SEA

Abu Simbel •

NUBIA

THE HISTORICAL BACKGROUND

Ancient Egyptian civilization grew and flourished thanks to the unique physical conditions of the country. Egypt is divided into two parts. The southern half, known as Upper Egypt, consists of a long narrow strip of fertile land on either side of the river Nile, which flows from south to north.

The rest of the land in Upper Egypt consists of desert. There are rocky mountains in the east, between the Nile and the Red Sea, and desert in the west, with a few oases. The northern half of the country, known as Lower Egypt, is flat land where the Nile divides into smaller branches that spread out into a wide V shape. This area is called the Nile Delta.

THE DUAL LAND

This idea of two halves making a whole was a common one in ancient Egyptian thought, with the country divided into north and south, and also into the black fertile land for living on and farming, which was called *kemet*, and the red desert, which was called *deshret*.

Egyptian rulers, who are known as pharaohs, were always called the kings of two lands, and the royal headdress was actually made up of two different crowns—the White Crown of Upper Egypt and the Red Crown of Lower Egypt.

The term "pharaoh" comes from the ancient Egyptian term *per-aa*, or "great house," which was the name for the Egyptian king's palace.

The Egyptian year was divided into three seasons, called inundation (June to September), cultivation (September to April), and harvest (April to June). The inundation, or flooding, occurred when the Nile increased in volume because of heavy rain from farther south in Africa. As the level of the Nile rose, it burst its banks all along the Nile Valley and flooded the surrounding countryside.

This wall carving shows the gods Seth and Horus, who represented Upper and Lower Egypt, tying a knot around the heiroglyph for union.

GOVERNMENT

The pharaoh was the most powerful member of society and was in charge of all religious and political institutions. He selected all the members of the government and all the important priests, who were often members of his own family. The office of king was also considered divine, with the king representing a god called Horus who was the son of two important gods, Osiris and Isis.

One of the pharaoh's titles was Son of Ra, showing that the king was also closely associated with the sun god Ra. In a spiritual sense, the main role of the king was to maintain *Maat*, which is hard to translate exactly, but includes the ideas of order as opposed to chaos, and a general sense of rightness.

Great emphasis was always placed on the importance of the union of the two lands, and this indicates that it was important for the efficient running of the state. The dual nature was almost always respected, with the employment of two *viziers* (secretaries of state), two treasurers, and sometimes even two civil services. The success of this strategy is shown by the fact that the country remained united for most of Egyptian history.

RELIGION

Religion and ritual occupied an important place in the lives of most ancient Egyptians. Even the poorest houses contained little shrines to one or more gods, often those concerned with domestic issues such as health and childbirth. The king and the government paid for the construction of fine temples in cities throughout the country. These temples were dedicated to the local gods of each area and to important national gods such as Ra, Osiris, and Amen. Access to these buildings was severely restricted, but there were many religious festivals throughout the year where statues or icons of the gods were carried through the streets by groups of priests. Many priests worked on a part-time basis, usually for one month a year. Full-time professional priests were devoted to the maintenance of the cults of each of the gods. Priests were not a separate segment of society. They married and had children, and lived in villages and towns with the rest of the community.

EGYPTIAN HISTORY

Ahmose I was the first pharaoh of the Eighteenth Dynasty and also the first pharaoh

A wall painting of workers making mortar for construction, taken from the tomb of Rekhmire, a governor of Thebes

to rule in the New Kingdom. This was the period when the boundaries of Egypt's empire and international influence reached their greatest extent. Egyptian history is divided into different periods by scholars in order to make it easier to understand. The first person to do this was an Egyptian priest called Manetho, who wrote a history of Egypt, in Greek, for the pharaoh Ptolemy I in about 300 BC. He divided the kings of Egypt into thirty different groups called dynasties. The divisions were usually based on different ruling families. Longer time periods are also marked off. The main ones are called the Old Kingdom (approximately 2600–2100 BC), the Middle Kingdom (approximately 2000–1600 BC) and the New Kingdom (approximately 1550–1090 BC).

There were also periods in Egyptian history when royal authority weakened, central government ceased to rule effectively, and the country broke down into smaller states run by local chiefs or warlords. These are called the Intermediate Periods. After the death of the last pharaoh of the Sixth Dynasty of the Old Kingdom, in approximately 2180 BC, parts of Egypt were run by rulers from different cities. Centers of power included Memphis, which was

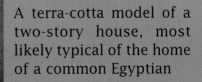

A terra-cotta model of a two-story house, most likely typical of the home of a common Egyptian

the Old Kingdom capital at the junction between the Nile Valley and the Nile Delta; Herakleopolis Magna near the Faiyum; and Thebes in the south. This time is known as the First Intermediate Period. After approximately 100 years, a Theban king called Nebhepetre Montuhotep II, who ruled between 2055 BC and 2004 BC, gained control of the entire country and the Middle Kingdom began.

MIDDLE KINGDOM

Nebhepetre Montuhotep II was succeeded by two short-lived rulers also called Montuhotep, and these three together are known as the kings of the Eleventh Dynasty. In 1985 BC, the last of them, Nebtawyra Montuhotep IV, was succeeded by Amenemhat I, who became the first king, or pharaoh, of the Twelfth Dynasty. Amenemhat was the son of a priest called Senusret and his wife Nofret, and was probably not related to the ruling family. However, he was a vizier for Nebtawyra Montuhotep IV, who seems to have had no natural heir. The change in dynasty is therefore a reflection of the new royal family.

Amenemhat I moved the home of the court north to a newly established town that he

A sculpture carved from black granite of the pharaoh Amenemhat III depicted as a sphinx with a lion's mane

called Amenemhat-Itjtawy, which means "Amenemhat takes possession of the Two Lands." The royal residence remained there until the end of the Middle Kingdom. The site of this town is not known, but modern scholars think that it was located somewhere near Amenemhat's pyramid at el-Lisht.

The administrative capital remained at Memphis in the north. Egypt flourished for the next 400 years. Pharaohs were buried in large pyramid complexes around the Faiyum, and the Faiyum area was developed with new towns and farms. Beautiful stone temples were built at important religious centers throughout Egypt, including the homes of the creator god Ptah at Memphis, the crocodile god Sobek at Medinet Maadi, Osiris, the god of death and the afterlife, at Abydos, and Amen, "the Hidden One," at Thebes. The political system of the country was modernized with local governors, or *nomarchs*, employed to run the forty-two *nomes*, or provinces, that the country was divided into. The Middle Kingdom pharaohs also annexed part of Nubia, which was the country immediately south of Egypt. Nubia occupied what is modern-day Sudan as well as the southern part of Egypt now submerged under Lake Nasser.

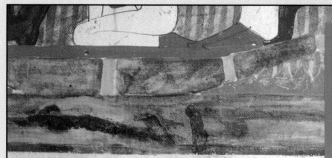

Servants carry offerings of food to the table, in this painting from the tomb of Nakht, a priest and astronomer who served the pharaoh Thutmose IV.

Egypt had been trading with Nubia since predynastic times, when the Egyptians wanted the luxury goods native to that country, including gold, ivory, and ebony. Middle Kingdom pharaohs supervised the construction of fortresses with names like, "Warding off the Blows" and "Curbing the Countries," which were built to guard passage along the Nile River. The main fortress was built at Buhen, which was located on the west bank of the Nile 160 miles upriver from Aswan.

By the time of the Thirteenth Dynasty (approximately 1790–1640 BC) royal power was in decline once more. There were a large number of short-lived rulers and a lack of political stability. Egypt's control of her new province in Nubia was weakened, and large numbers of Asiatic people from Canaan and Syria came to live in the eastern part of the delta. Eventually even the new city at Itjtawy was abandoned. The period between 1640 and 1550 BC is called the Second Intermediate Period.

FOREIGN RULERS

In approximately 1640 BC a new city was founded at a site in the eastern part of the delta known today as Tell el-Daba. The city was called Avaris, and it was the capital of a new group of rulers who made up the Fifteenth Dynasty. For the first time in its history Egypt was ruled in part by foreigners, as the Fifteenth Dynasty pharaohs were actually a group of people known as the Hyksos.

Modern scholars disagree as to the origin of the Hyksos. They may have been made up of groups of Asiatic people who were already living in the area when central control broke down, and who gradually took power as they began to outnumber the native Egyptians. They may also have been a new group of people who invaded Egypt from Canaan, to the east.

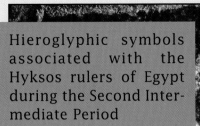

Hieroglyphic symbols associated with the Hyksos rulers of Egypt during the Second Inter-mediate Period

The only written source for the arrival of the Hyksos in Egypt comes from Manetho, who was writing over a thousand years after the events. He wrote that "invaders of an obscure race marched in confidence of victory against our land," and described how they "burned our cities ruthlessly, razed to the ground the temples of the gods, and treated all the natives with cruel hostility." Archaeological evidence from the site of Avaris shows very different architectural and burial practices from the Egyptian ways at this time, and indicates that the Hyksos were very similar to, if not the same as, peoples living in Canaan and Syria.

During the Second Intermediate Period the Hyksos kings ruled most of the the northern half of the country, including the eastern delta, Memphis, and probably as far south as Hermopolis. At the same time, rule of the southern half of the country was centered around Thebes, where local chieftains, known as the Seventeenth Dynasty, ruled between Aswan in the south and Meir (also known as Cusae) in the north. We know very little about the Fourteenth and Sixteenth Dynasties, which seem to have been minor kings ruling small parts of Egypt at the same time.

Nubia, to the south of Egypt, was divided into three areas. Wawat, or "Lower Nubia," was the areas of land surrounding the river Nile stretching south from Aswan, and the first cataract of the Nile to the second cataract. Kush, or "Upper Nubia," was located between the second and fourth cataracts, and "Southern Nubia" lay between the fourth and sixth cataracts toward the modern Sudanese capital city, Khartoum. Cataracts are outcrops of granite that create rapids and make it impossible to travel on a river except at times of high water. During the Second Intermediate Period, the series of fortresses that had been built by the Middle Kingdom pharaohs around the second cataract were conquered by Nubian rulers based at the city of Kerma in Kush.

During this time, therefore, Egypt was divided into three main areas ruled by three different powerful families, one Asiatic in origin, one Egyptian, and one Nubian. In theory the whole of Egypt was under the control of the Hyksos rulers. However, the Theban chieftains became increasingly reluctant to deal with these "foreigners." A war of independence was begun by the fourteenth ruler of the Seventeenth Dynasty, a man called King Seqenenre Ta'a II, who came to power in 1560 BC.

Seqenenre Ta'a was the son of Seqenenre Ta'a I and his wife Tetisheri, and he was married to his sister Ahhotep. They had two sons called Kamose and Ahmose. Seqenenre Ta'a and his family lived at Thebes, and in theory were supposed to show obedience to the Hyksos king, Apophis, in the north.

The relationship between the two royal houses is illustrated by a story dating from the Rameses period called "The Quarrel of Apophis and Seqenenre." It starts by describing the power of Apophis, saying that "he had put the entire land under taxation." The story goes on to describe a meeting between Apophis and his advisers. The Hyksos king seems to have been determined to provoke the Thebans for some reason, and so he decided to send them a ridiculous demand. This took the form of a complaint that the hippopotamuses in a pool at Thebes were disturbing the Hyksos king's sleep, even though they were actually hundreds of miles away. "When the messenger of King Apophis arrived at the southern city [Thebes], he was taken into the presence of the ruler of the southern city. Then they said to the messenger of the King Apophis, 'Why have you been sent to the southern city? Why have you made this journey?' Then the messenger said, 'King Apophis

An ancient Egyptian model of a hippopotamus

sends to you, saying "Do away with the hippopotamus-pool, which is on the east of the city, for they prevent me sleeping day and night.'" Then the ruler of the southern city was silent for a long time; and he found himself unable to answer the messenger of King Apophis." Sadly the end of the story is lost, and

we don't know what reply Seqenenre Ta'a and his advisers sent back.

This story indicates that the Hyksos king was determined to bully the rulers at Thebes, and also to remind them that he was in charge of Egypt. It may have been this, or other similarly unreasonable requests, that finally prompted Seqenenre Ta'a to rebel. However, it is also important to remember that, on a more philosophical level, the Egyptians felt that it was against the natural order of things, or Maat, for Egypt to be ruled by foreigners. Asiatics and Nubians had traditionally been seen as Egypt's enemies.

THE THEBAN REVOLT

Seqenenre Ta'a began a campaign of revolt against the northern rulers. We have no record of specific battles between the two powers, but

Seqenenre Ta'a does not appear to have been particularly successful. We do know that after only a few years, when still in his early thirties, he died a gruesome death in battle. This is because his mummy shows horrific wounds to his head and neck that match exactly the size and shape of typical Canaanite weapons, including ax heads, indicating that he was clubbed, stabbed with daggers, and axed to death. It also appears that his body had begun to decompose before he was mummified, suggesting that it may have lain on the battlefield for some time before being recovered for burial.

His tomb has not yet been identified, although it is known to be somewhere in western Thebes. During the Third Intermediate Period many of the royal mummies from the West Bank at Thebes were taken away from their tombs and hidden together in a tomb near Deir el-Bahri. These were discovered in 1881, and the mummy of Seqenenre Ta'a was found among them.

KING KAMOSE

Seqenenre Ta'a was succeeded by his eldest son, Kamose, in 1555 BC. At this time Kamose was still a teenager and his younger brother

Ahmose was a small child. The rebellion led under his father Seqenenre Ta'a II appears to have been squashed, and a treaty was drawn up between Apophis and Kamose. From their base in the delta, the Hyksos were able to control the land and sea trade routes between Egypt, the east Mediterranean, and the Near East.

Sculpture of Kamose, brother of Ahmose and pharaoh before him

In Nubia, to the south, the Kush rulers were able to control all the trade coming up from Africa into Egypt, including the most important resource, gold. The Hyksos rulers had formed an alliance with the kings of Kush, bypassing the Egyptians in the middle by using a travel route through the oases to the west of the Nile Valley. This meant that the Theban rulers in the middle could be cut out of any trade deals. They would not have been able to sell their products, such as papyrus, linen, or stone vessels, and would

have been unable to obtain important foreign products they relied on, including incense from Africa to burn in temple ceremonies and timber from Syria needed for their building projects.

An important historical document was found written on two stone monuments in the great Karnak Temple to the god Amen in Thebes. These are called the Kamose *stelae*, and they record the official position that the treaty was a good one for the Theban kingdom. "We are doing alright in our part of Egypt. Their free land is cultivated for us, and our cattle graze in the delta grasslands, while corn is sent for our pigs. Our cattle have not been seized."

However, Kamose was not prepared to continue showing obedience to the Hyksos kings, and probably in his third year of rule, 1553 BC, he launched a surprise attack to the north.

Kamose's army contained both native Egyptian fighters and troops from Wawat,

Wooden models of the pleasure boats used to transport the nobility in Egypt

known as the Medjay. who were originally nomadic tribespeople who had moved north to live in Egypt during the Middle Kingdom. They were famous for their fighting skills, and they were especially skilled with the bow and arrow.

The Kamose stelae record the swift progress of the king's army as it headed down river in a flotilla of boats, propelled by sails when the wind was in the right direction and by teams of rowers when the wind failed. "I sailed north in my might to repel the Hyksos through the command of Amen, with my brave army before me like a flame of fire and the Medjay archers on top of our cabin roofs on the lookout for the Asiatics in order to destroy their places."

The Egyptian army seems to have had little trouble subduing the towns between the Theban kingdom's frontier at Cusae and the old Egyptian capital at Memphis. Kamose was intent both on beating the Hyksos and also on punishing Egyptians who had collaborated with them. This seems rather unfair, as many Egyptians living under Hyksos rule would have had little say in the matter. Kamose made a particular example of a man called Tety, son of Pepy, who lived in the town of Nefrusy, which was somewhere north of Cusae. "I was not going to let him escape, once I had repelled the Asiatics who had defiled Egypt, so that he could turn Nefrusy into a nest of Asiatics. I passed the night in my ship, my heart happy; and when day dawned I was upon him as if I was a hawk. When breakfast came I overthrew him, having destroyed his walls and slaughtered his people and made his wife come down to the river bank [as a prisoner]."

Other cities along the banks of the Nile were treated in a similar manner. As news spread of the approach of Kamose's army, some people even ran away from their towns. Kamose and his army then sailed up along the eastern side of the delta toward the Hyksos capital at Avaris. Kamose was enjoying his successes, and he used psychological warfare in addition to brute force in order to terrify people as he passed by. The Kamose stelae record his words as he shouted, "Look behind you! My troops are a threat behind you. The women of Avaris shall not conceive, and their hearts shall not beat in the midst of their bodies, when the war-whoop of my troops is heard!"

THE BATTLE AT AVARIS

Kamose and his army apparently reached Avaris practically unopposed. Avaris was the capital of the Fifteenth Dynasty rulers and the stronghold of the Hyksos. It was built on a series of small islands and neighboring shores next to the Nile. Here, Kamose and his army found a heavily fortified citadel strategically

A wall carving of
Egyptian soldiers

placed at a bend in the river and surrounded by a mud brick wall nearly thirty feet wide and at least as high. The wall was lined with buttresses and watchtowers from which Hyksos soldiers kept an eye on the harbors, the river, and the rest of the countryside. In the Hyksos citadel there was a large palace for the rulers, gardens full of trees, smaller houses, and offices.

The town of Avaris spread around the citadel and included houses, shops, and temples to Canaanite and Egyptian gods. One such temple was over ninety yards long and painted blue. The town was one of the biggest cities in the eastern Mediterranean at this time, and was a center of international trade and learning. Rather than having separate cemeteries, the

The Rhind Papyrus, which was found in the ruins at Avaris, dates from the time of the Hyksos rulers of Egypt. In hieratic, the written form of hieroglyphics, it tells us much about ancient Egyptian mathematics.

citizens of Avaris were buried under their own houses, with children first placed inside Canaanite amphorae, which are large two-handled jars. Other non-Egyptian practices included donkey burials, where pairs of animals were sacrificed and interred in front of temples. As well as having the advantage of being inside a highly fortified city, the Hyksos soldiers were also better equipped than their Egyptian enemies, possessing the latest weapons and armor from Canaan and Syria, including axes like those that had killed Seqenenre Ta'a, horse-drawn chariots, and body armor.

Kamose and his followers came to a halt and took stock of their situation. "I made the mighty transport boat beach at the edge of cultivation, with the fleet behind it, as the sparrow hawk lands on the flats of Avaris!" The inhabitants of the city looked nervously out at the army gathered outside their walls. "I espied his women upon his roof, peering out of their windows toward the harbor. Their bellies stirred not as they saw me, peeping from their loopholes in their walls like the young of rats in their holes, saying 'he is swift!'"

Kamose and his army took possession of a large fleet of trading ships anchored in the harbor. "I haven't left a plank to the hundreds of ships of fresh cedar which were filled with gold, lapis lazuli, silver, turquoise, bronze axes without number, oil, incense, fat, honey, willow, box wood, and all their fine woods—all fine products of Syria—I have confiscated all of it."

After this raid was successfully completed, however, Kamose seems to have reached a stalemate with the occupants of the city. He and his armies were outside the walls looking up, and the Hyksos were inside looking down. The Hyksos showed no inclination to come out and engage with their enemy, and the Egyptian army was not strong enough or well-equipped enough to storm Avaris itself.

THE SOUTHERN ALLIES

Apophis, the ruler of the Hyksos, then tried a cunning plan. He sent a messenger carrying a letter to the ruler of Kush in the south. Unfortunately for the Hyksos, however, the man was captured in one of the oases by Kamose's troops. The document was found to contain an invitation from Apophis to the Kushites suggesting that they should attack the Theban area from the south. In the letter, Apophis begins by listing his grievances against Egypt. "Do you see what Egypt has done to me? The ruler of the place, Kamose, is pushing me off my own ground. I have not attacked him in any way comparable to all that he has done to you. He chooses to plague these two lands, mine and yours, and he has hacked them up!" This passage indicates that Kamose had previously executed raids into Nubia in order to try to win back the territories of Wawat lost at the end of the Middle Kingdom. Apophis then continues, "Come north! Do not hold back! See, he is here with me. There is none who will stand up to you in Egypt. See, I will not give him a way out until you arrive! Then we shall divide the towns of Egypt, and Kush shall be in joy." Kamose ordered that the letter be sent back to Apophis in order to show him that his plan had failed. "I had it taken back that it might be returned to him again. My victory astounded him and his limbs were wracked!"

After some time had passed with no decisive movement on either side, the Theban army decided to retire. Hurling insults up at the occupants of the Hyksos city as they left, Kamose and his army returned to Thebes in triumph. Kamose describes this return trip in glowing terms.

"What a happy home-trip for the Ruler with his army ahead of him! They had no casualties, nor did anyone blame his fellow, nor did their hearts weep! I moored on home soil during the season of inundation. Everyone was bright eyed, the land had abundant food, the river bank was resplendent! Thebes was festive, women and men came out to see me. Every woman hugged her neighbor, no one was tearful."

Another mission carried out in 1553 BC ensured that the oases to the west of the Theban region were secure, and also that the traditional north–south oases route could no longer be used for communication between Avaris to the north and Kush to the south. The Kamose stelae records the following: "I sent a strong troop overland to destroy the Bahariya Oasis, while I was in Sako [approximately seventy miles south of Herakleopolis] in order to prevent rebels from being behind me."

Although the Hyksos had not been defeated or driven out of Egypt, a great deal had been achieved. Communication between the Hyksos and their Nubian allies had been severed. Many of their territories north of Hermopolis had been captured by the Theban army. Equally important, Kamose had demonstrated that the Hyksos were not invincible and that they could be beaten. The power of the Hyksos had been reduced throughout Egypt, and their one remaining stronghold was their eastern delta capital at Avaris.

Kamose died in 1550 BC, leaving no sons. We do not know if he died of natural causes or war wounds, but he was only about twenty-five years old at the time of his death. He was buried in a tomb with a small pyramid on top in a cemetery at Dra Abu el-Naga, on the West Bank at Thebes. His coffin was discovered in 1857, but unfortunately his mummified body disintegrated as soon as the coffin was opened. Kamose was succeeded by his younger brother Ahmose, who was probably less than ten years old at the time.

KING AHMOSE

We know very little about the child-hood of this new ruler of the Theban kingdom. Ahmose almost certainly lived at Thebes with his mother Ahhotep and his grand-mother Tetisheri, and it is clear that he was very attached to both women. He had at least one sister, called Ahmose Nefertari, who would later become his wife.

It is possible that Ahmose spent some time at Elkab, about forty miles south of Luxor, with the family of the rulers of the city who had remained loyal to the Theban cause. There he would have gone to school to learn read-ing and writing, and would also have been tutored in the art of war.

Ahmose also visited a new settlement built by Seqenenre Ta'a II at a site called Deir el-Ballas, about thirty miles north of Thebes. The

32191.

major buildings there included a palace for the Theban rulers known today as the Northern Palace, large houses for their advisers, communal kitchens, and a fortress or large watchtower built on a platform, known today as the Southern Palace. The walls of these buildings were decorated with suitably warlike themes including pictures of battle axes. This site had been used as a staging post during previous conflicts.

Ahmose's mother, Ahhotep, had to act as regent while her son was still a child. This meant that she used all her experience to help him rule until he was old enough to manage by himself. A stele later erected by Ahmose in the main temple to the god Amen at Karnak describes her role: "She is one who has accomplished the rites and cared for Egypt. She has looked after Egypt's troops and she has guarded them. She has brought back the fugitives and collected together the deserters. She has pacified Upper Egypt and expelled her rebels." This passage indicates that Ahhotep played a military role unusual for a royal mother. She also set a precedent for the early New Kingdom, when other royal women would also have significant and powerful political roles.

PREPARATIONS FOR WAR

For the first few years of Ahmose's reign, work at Thebes was concentrated on building up the army and its equipment. Kamose's battle at Avaris had shown the Thebans that their weaponry was not strong enough to take on fortified Hyksos cities. Essentially, the Hyksos had been able to dominate Egypt because they had better weapons and superior military technology, which had originally been developed in Canaan and Syria. The Theban army now needed to learn how to make and use similar weapons. Equipment that had been captured in battle was carefully studied, and skilled craftsmen from Canaan and Syria were almost certainly employed to teach the Theban armorers.

Important innovations included the horse-drawn chariot, a new form of bow called a composite bow, body armor, and a more effective dagger. The chariots needed to be both light and strong. Egyptian chariots were constructed from locally available acacia wood and leather. They consisted of a wooden semicircular framework with an open back that sat on an axle holding two wheels. The wheels were about three feet in diameter, with four or six spokes and leather tires. A long pole was attached to the center of the axle and two horses were harnessed to the front end. Each chariot was manned by a driver and a soldier. The soldier carried a shield, a spear, and a bow and arrow. They were sometimes accompanied by a runner, who had the dangerous job of fighting off anyone attacking the chariot. Chariots were very useful for rushing at the enemy and breaking up infantry formations, as mobile firing platforms, and for chasing anyone running away. They were also an obvious status symbol for young men, and chariots quickly became the prized possessions of the aristocratic warrior class.

Bows and arrows had long been a crucial element in warfare, providing armies with a long-range assault weapon. The traditional Egyptian bow was a simple weapon made of a wooden rod, usually between three feet and six feet long, and strung with twisted animal gut. Arrows were made of reeds with three feathers and a bronze or hard stone point at the tip. The new composite bow used by the Hyksos had originated in Mesopotamia (modern Iraq). It was a formidable weapon with far greater power, range, and accuracy than anything known up to that time. It was also much smaller than the bow traditionally used by

Egyptian soldiers, which meant that it was the ideal weapon to be used from a chariot. A composite bow was formed by gluing strips of wood, goat horn, and sinew together. This made it more elastic and able to propel arrows a much greater distance. Archers needed to have special training to handle these new weapons. They were also given thick bracelets or armlets made of leather to protect their arms from the kick of the string.

Body armor was also worn for the first time by the Egyptian soldiers. The armor consisted of rows of small metal discs sewn onto leather or linen jackets. A new form of dagger was introduced as well. This consisted of a long narrow blade and a *tang* (the piece going into the handle) cast all in one piece. Another dagger with a curved blade, called a *khepresh*, was also copied from the Hyksos. Egyptian axes were also modernized. In the Old and Middle Kingdoms the ax consisted of a semicircular copper head tied to a wooden handle by cords. The Middle Kingdom also saw the introduction of an ax with a longer blade, and another with a curved blade and three prongs or tangs at the back that went into the handle. Now the Egyptians developed an ax with a longer, thinner straight blade made of bronze and designed to penetrate body armor. Spears designed for throwing or stabbing the enemy were also given bronze tips. Specially trained armorers and woodworkers were put to work to produce all the new weapons.

METALWORKING

Bronze was made from mixing copper and tin. However, it was difficult for the Theban forces to gain access to new supplies of these materials, as copper was traditionally mined in the Sinai Desert, which was under Hyksos control, and tin was probably imported from Syria. Most of the material used was found by recycling existing metal objects such as pots and pans and other, less efficient metal weapons. Bronze was better than copper because, as an alloy of copper and tin, it is a much stronger metal, and also it melts at a lower temperature than copper alone, which means that it is easier to work with.

The first stage in the production of bronze weapons was to melt the metal. Metals were usually traded around the Mediterranean in the form of large ingots shaped like cakes, buns, or sometimes a specific shape for carrying in an oxhide. Together with metal household objects

A gold breastplate showing the pharaoh Ahmose being purified by sacred water from the gods Amen Re and Ra

and other scraps, these ingots were placed into large crucibles (clay pots) over a charcoal fire. Rows of men then blew into the fire through clay blowpipes in order to fan the flames. Bellows were not commonly used until later in the New Kingdom. Once melted, the bronze was poured into smaller containers or molds, to produce either smaller portions of metal to work with, or finished objects. Once the metal had cooled down and solidified, blacksmiths could then hammer the bronze into the required shape, using large flat stones as anvils and smaller, rounded stones as hammers. Smaller objects such as spears and arrowheads could be made by pouring molten bronze straight into carved stone molds.

MILITARY CAMPAIGNS

By 1540 BC, Ahmose was considered old enough to begin his own military campaign to finally rid the country of the hated Hyksos. Unfortunately, we have no record like that of the Kamose stelae to describe his campaign. However, we do have evidence from biographical inscriptions carved on the walls of the tombs of two of his strongest allies, from the town of Elkab. Both Ahmose, son of Abana, and Ahmose Pennekheb fought for Ahmose's army. These men were the same age as Ahmose and they had almost certainly all grown up together.

The walls of the tomb chapels of these two allies are decorated with "tomb autobiographies." These are the life stories of individuals spelled out on the walls of their tombs so that the gods can see how successful they have been in their lives and careers. Ahmose, son of Abana, was a naval officer, and his narrative shows that he came from a military family: "I had my upbringing in the town of Nekheb [Elkab], my father being a soldier of the king of Upper and Lower Egypt . . . Then I became a soldier in his stead on the ship called *The Wild Bull* in the reign of the Lord of the Two Lands Nebpehtyre (Ahmose) . . ." His close relationship to the young ruler is indicated in the next passage: "I was then taken on the ship called *The Northern* on account of my bravery; and I used to attend the king . . . when he went forth in his chariot."

We also have one small piece of evidence of the war between the Thebans and the Hyksos from someone actually based inside the Hyksos capital. Avaris had been a civilized, international city and a center of learning. A famous historical document called the Rhind Historical Papyrus was written there in about 1550 BC. This contains a series of mathematical problems and solutions, including how to work out the volumes of rectangles, triangles, and pyramids, and how to work with fractions. There is also a small piece of text on the back of the papyrus written during the reign of Apophis by someone who felt he should record the important events of the time.

This papyrus states that in the eleventh year of Ahmose's reign he entered the city of Heliopolis. In the same year, he also entered the city of Sile. This shows that Ahmose moved relatively quickly, capturing Heliopolis, just north of Memphis, in early July, and then bypassing Avaris to capture the frontier settlement at Sile in mid-October. This made good tactical sense, because by taking Sile, Ahmose was effectively cutting off any hope that the Hyksos rulers may have had of being reinforced by troops from Canaan. He was also severing the communication links between the Hyksos and their allies, essentially isolating them at Avaris. Ahmose and his armies then advanced to Avaris itself.

THE SECOND BATTLE AT AVARIS

Like Kamose before him, Ahmose finally reached the Hyksos capital at Avaris. To begin with, his armies were no more successful than his brother's had been. Ahmose's troops camped around the outside of the fortified city. Ahmose, son of Abana, said that "Siege was laid at the town of Avaris, and I continued in my brave acts as foot soldier in his majesty's presence." Skirmishes broke out between the opposing forces. "Then there was combat on the water in the canal of Avaris, and I made a capture and brought a hand. It was reported to the king's herald, and then I was given the Gold of Valor." The Egyptians tended to keep count of the number of enemies killed in battle by chopping off their enemies' hands or sometimes their penises and then counting the piles of body parts. The Gold of Valor was the highest military honor awarded in battle and it took the form of a gold collar. Ahmose, son of Abana, was eventually awarded seven of these gold collars.

War raged for some time around the city, with Ahmose, son of Abana, involved in at least two more battles. "Then there was renewed combat in this location, and I made

Wooden model figures of Egyptian infantry on the march

another capture there, and brought a hand, and then I was given the Gold of Valor again. Then there was combat on Egyptian soil south of this town, and I brought off one captive." Eventually the Theban troops were victorious and were able to capture the city. Ahmose, son of Abana, records this almost as an afterthought with the simple sentence, "Then Avaris was sacked."

Archaeological evidence indicates that the whole town was occupied by Ahmose's victorious army, which Manetho later said contained 48,000 soldiers. Important buildings and temples were ransacked and many were burned to the ground. The armies set up camp in a series of tents for the Theban soldiers and their Medjay allies, and army kitchens were quickly set up to feed the tired troops. There are a number of single and group graves of young men at the site, some containing incomplete bodies, indicating that many of the Hyksos were quickly disposed of. Others were captured and turned into servants for the Egyptian troops.

Ahmose, son of Abana, boasts of such a transaction: "One man and three women, total four heads; and his majesty granted me them as servants." We do not know whether the rest of the Hyksos escaped or were freed, but we know that some

of the Hyksos and their followers fled across the Sinai Desert into Canaan, where they took refuge south of Gaza in a fortress at Sharuhen.

Ahmose then decided to rebuild parts of the city at Avaris in an Egyptian style. He commissioned two buildings very similar to the Northern Palace and Southern Palace at Deir el-Ballas. These became the campaign residences of Ahmose and his armies.

Wooden models of Nubian archers

Manetho later wrote of the Hyksos that, "Giving up the siege, they made a treaty to the effect that they should all quit Egypt and go unharmed wherever they wished." But it is clear that Ahmose was not prepared to allow the Hyksos to regroup and rearm once more in Canaan.

Sharuhen was a fortified city similar to Avaris and had been an important power base for the Hyksos in Canaan. It was a rich city, and many hoards of gold have been found in excavations of the site, which is known today as Tell el-'Ajjul.

Ahmose saw the presence of Hyksos forces so close to the borders of Egypt as a continued threat. He decided to pursue them further in order to gain a final, decisive victory. For the next three years he and his armies marched across the Sinai Desert and besieged the city of Sharuhen in a series of campaigns, eventually capturing and destroying the city in 1335 BC. Ahmose, son of Abana, wrote, "Sharuhen was besieged over three years, and then his majesty sacked it, and I brought off booty from there, two women and one hand. Then I was given the Gold of Valor, and I was granted the booty as servants." Further expeditions marched farther north toward Syria, probably chasing the stragglers of the Hyksos army.

Egypt was now unified under a strong king for the first time in more than 100 years. Later historians record a change of dynasty at this time, with Ahmose becoming the first pharaoh of the Eighteenth Dynasty and the first pharaoh of the New Kingdom.

A wooden statuette of Nefertari, sister and wife of Ahmose

However, there was no room for complacency. Egypt's aggressive expeditions into Canaan had committed the country to a military pattern that would be followed throughout the New Kingdom. The Egyptian empire now included areas of south Canaan that acted as a buffer zone to protect the country from any other Asiatic power. This new territory had to be maintained and defended by all future rulers, essentially turning Egypt into a military superpower. Such campaigns would eventually develop into wars of conquest under later pharaohs such as Thutmose III and Rameses II, when large areas of Canaan and Syria came under Egyptian control.

INTERNATIONAL DIPLOMACY

Recent archaeological evidence unearthed at Avaris indicates that Ahmose may have found an important ally in his fight against the Hyksos. Many thousands of fragments of wall paintings have been discovered that were originally in the new palace built by Ahmose at Avaris. These are brightly colored and very beautiful, but completely un-Egyptian in style and subject matter. Scenes show people involved in various sporting and ritual activities, including acrobatics and wrestling, and men leaping over bulls. There are also pictures of mountain goats, antelopes, leopards, and lions, as well as paintings of trees and plants and watery landscapes. The scenes have been recognized as typical of paintings known from royal palaces in Crete, which was occupied at this time by people called the Minoans. Bull leaping had a special ritual significance for the Minoans and seems to have been part of a ceremony that showed human dominance over the power of animals. However, it should be remembered that there are almost no written records from Minoan Crete, and no one is sure of the exact meaning of these pictures.

These and other scenes uncovered at Avaris are usually only found in royal palaces in Crete during this period. We may conclude that Minoan artists must have visited Ahmose's new palace at Avaris. It is possible that these types of wall decorations were very fashionable at the time, and this is why Ahmose wanted them. However, it is more likely that these paintings are evidence of an alliance between Ahmose and the rulers of Crete. Such an alliance between the royal courts of Egypt and Crete would have been advantageous to both. Crete was the strongest naval power at the time, and Cretan ships could have protected the Egyptian coast against invasion from the sea. In exchange, Ahmose could offer gold and other luxury products to the Minoan rulers and their craftsmen. Another suggestion has been put forward by the archaeologist Manfred Bietak, who is in charge of the excavations at Avaris. He believes that Ahmose married a Minoan princess, and that these pictures decorated her new home in the Egyptian delta.

THE NUBIAN CAMPAIGN

With the northern borders of Egypt made secure, Ahmose turned his attention to the south, where the former Egyptian territory of Wawat and most of the rest of Nubia were still under the control of the king of Kush, who had been an ally of the Hyksos. The Nubian rulers, and the Nubian population in general, were often portrayed by the Egyptians as backward and barbaric. In reality the Kushite culture was a highly developed one, with a strong economic base, good resources (especially gold), and highly developed religious and political systems. The Kushite capital was at the city of Kerma, located between the third and fourth cataracts of the Nile River. Surrounded by massive fortifications with walls at least thirty-three feet high, Kerma contained a massive royal palace, a large temple, and a circular audience hall, as well as many houses and gardens. Occupants in the city included the king of Kush and his family, the court and government officials, officers and soldiers who defended the town, priests, and many workers and servants.

There was a vast cemetery nearby that contained the tombs of Kush's rulers. Kushite burial customs were different from those of the Egyptians. Important individuals were buried on wooden beds, and were often supplied with a box containing items for personal care for use in the afterlife such as bronze razors and stone vessels for eye makeup. Many men were also buried with swords. The kings of Kush were buried in large round mounds known as *tumuli*, which are about 12 feet high and nearly 300 feet across. Each tumulus contained the bodies of the king and his closest and most important officials. Sometimes the tombs also contained the bodies of hundreds of servants who were human sacrifices at the time of the king's burial. These people included servants, guards, and women to act as sexual partners for the king in his afterlife.

The stele of the
Nubians

At some point after 1335 BC, Ahmose and his army sailed south to face the Nubians. For this war he left behind his Medjay troops, as he was uncertain how they would act if faced with members of their own tribes on the opposing side. Ahmose, son of Abana, reported that the king "ascended the river to Kush to destroy the Nubian Bowmen. His majesty made great slaughter among them, and I brought booty from there; two living men and three hands. Then I was rewarded with gold once again, and two female slaves were given to me. His majesty journeyed north, his heart rejoicing in valor and victory. He had conquered southerners and northerners."

Although Ahmose had won back the Egyptian territory of Wawat between the first and second cataracts, there was still some resistance from the Nubian forces. A rebel called Aata attacked the Egyptian army somewhere north of the second cataract. Ahmose, son of Abana, described the event: "Then Aata came to the South (into Egypt). His fate brought on his doom. The gods of Upper Egypt grasped him. He was found by his majesty in Tenttaa. His majesty carried him off as a living captive and all his people as booty."

King Ahmose was faced by at least one more uprising within Egypt before the country was finally at peace. An Egyptian soldier called Tetian seems to have tried some sort of rebellion. Once more, Ahmose, son of Abana, described the scene: "Then came the enemy called Tetian. He had gathered the rebels to himself. His majesty slew him and his troops were wiped out. Then I was given three persons and five fields of land in my town." Ahmose had succeeded in restoring the northern and southern boundaries of Egypt, and the country was finally reunited under one pharaoh. He was now able to turn his attention to governing the land of Egypt itself.

GOVERNING THE COUNTRY

Ahmose's father, Seqenenre Ta'a, and his brother, Kamose, had both died or been killed when he was still a small child. Consequently his family life was dominated by his female relatives. His grandmother Tetisheri died, probably around 1541 BC, and although her body was found with the other royal mummies in the tomb near Deir-el Bahri, we do not know the exact site of her burial at Thebes.

Ahmose's mother, Ahhotep, had governed the Theban region with him throughout the years of military campaigns, and continued to help him once peace had been achieved. At some point during these years Ahmose married his sister Ahmose Nefertari. We know that she was very important to him. She gave birth to their son and Ahmose's heir, Amenhotep, and a daughter called Meritamen, who was later to become his wife.

In 1531 BC, Ahmose turned his attention to the government within Egypt. He set out to reorganize the systems of both national and local government. In times of peace the Egyptian state had always been good at maintaining social and economic control with an elaborate administrative infrastructure and a large civil service. During the Old Kingdom there were two main offices of state apart from the pharaoh, those of the vizier and the overseer of royal works. During the Middle Kingdom the country had functioned under a strong, centralized bureaucratic system made up of different government departments, including the treasury, the labor bureau, the fields bureau, and the war department. These all reported to the vizier, who in turn reported to the pharaoh.

During his many years of military campaigning, Ahmose left the domestic affairs of the Theban region in the hands of his mother, Ahhotep. Now, in peacetime, he was faced with the task of reconstructing the entire country after years of division and neglect.

With the victories over the Hyksos and the Kushites, he governed a country over twice the size of his original Theban kingdom.

GOD'S WIFE OF AMEN

Worship of the god Amen had originated in the Theban region. This god had risen in importance during the Middle Kingdom, as Thebes was the hometown of the Middle Kingdom pharaohs. The Theban kings from the Seventeenth Dynasty had also promoted the worship of Amen, and Ahmose also honored this god for the many victories he had achieved, endowing the main Amen temple at Karnak with many gifts.

Ahmose's first political acts were concerned with strengthening the role of the kingship and the royal family, as well as strengthening their relationship to this important god. Following the examples of Tetisheri and Ahhotep as strong royal women, Ahmose introduced the temple post of God's Wife of Amen to be given to the wife or daughter of the pharaoh. This was intended to then be handed down to each female heir. The functions of this job were to play the part of the wife of Amen in

religious ceremonies, which stressed the idea that the pharaohs were actually the children of the god and the royal wife. The post of God's Wife of Amen was a powerful one, and Ahmose also gave the recipient land to provide income through rents and produce, and a staff of male officials to administer the estates. Ahmose Nefertari was made the first God's Wife of Amen. She made a number of gifts to temples throughout Egypt, including those at Thebes, at Abydos, and at Serabit el-Khadim in the Sinai Desert, which was the main center of turquoise mining for Egypt.

Ahmose also rewarded members of his own family and the local rulers who had been loyal to the Theban kingdom by giving them land and property. This had the effect of tying them more firmly than ever to the crown. He also established a more centralized system of government, where officers, including the two viziers of Upper and Lower Egypt, reported directly to him.

New administrative posts were established in Nubia, including the office of the viceroy of Nubia, who reported directly to the pharaoh. The settlement at Buhen was extensively renovated and resettled, and a loyal subject called Turi was posted to the fort and

A painting of Egyptian wrestlers in various positions

appointed governor of Buhen. His main jobs were to collect taxes and to organize the administration of the Nubian goldmines that were once more under Egyptian control. Gold was usually extracted from veins found in quartz rocks. Fires were lit inside the mines that heated and cracked the face of the rock. Men then broke pieces off with hammers and picks. Lumps of rock were then carried outside the mine, where they were first crushed by large stone mortars and then ground into a fine powder. This powder was washed with water in shallow pans so that the fragments of gold, which were very heavy, sunk to the bottom of

A wooden model of a carpenter's workshop

the pan. These fragments were then collected and melted together into small ingots.

BUILDING PROJECTS

It was also important for Ahmose to rebuild and refurnish many of Egypt's great temples, which had been neglected and damaged during the Hyksos rule. The Hyksos had a habit of looting statues and carvings from temples and selling them to foreigners, and many Middle Kingdom examples have been found in Nubia and Canaan. An official called Neferperet was sent to reopen the limestone quarries at Tura, near Memphis. He left an inscription carved into the hillside above the quarry which reads, "The quarry chambers were opened anew; good limestone of Tura was taken out for his temples of millions of years, the Temple of Ptah, the Temple of Amen in Thebes, and all the monuments which his majesty made for the gods. The stone was dragged with oxen which his majesty captured in his victories among the Canaanites."

Ahmose's mother, Ahhotep, died around 1530 BC. He had lost not only his beloved mother but also one of his closest advisers, and Ahmose was determined that Ahhotep's burial would be a splendid one.

A tomb was prepared for her on the West Bank of Thebes at the site of Dra Abu el-Naga, and she was buried in a fantastic coffin and surrounded by many precious gifts. This burial site was discovered in 1859 by a French Egyptologist named Auguste Mariette. Modern rules for the conduct of excavations had not yet come into force, and an extraordinary tussle followed when various Egyptian officials fought over her body and all her funerary goods. Luckily for modern scholars, they all ended up in the Cairo Museum and are on display today.

A wooden model of a weaver's workshop

Ahhotep's body was placed in a *rishi* coffin, which was fashionable in the Seventeenth and early Eighteenth Dynasties. "Rishi" is the Arabic word for feathers, and it refers to the decoration that looks like a set of folded wings covering much of the lid of the wooden coffin. This probably symbolizes either the protective wings of the goddesses Isis and Nephthys, or possibly the soul of the dead person, which could be shown as a bird called a *Ba*. Ahhotep was buried with many beautiful pieces of jewelry and, unusual for a woman, with many weapons. These reflect the important role she had in governing Egypt and also the military nature of government at this time. Most of the goods in her tomb

Women applying perfume

were labeled with the names of Kamose and Ahmose and some may actually have once been their personal possessions. The quality of some of the objects is quite crude compared to similar Middle Kingdom examples, but they are still splendid in many ways. There are also some examples that look very similar to objects from Minoan Crete, which reinforces the idea that there were strong contacts between the two royal houses. The jewelry includes necklaces, pendants, bracelets, and armlets. There is also a famous necklace made up of three of the military decorations known as the Order of the Golden Fly. Weapons include a richly jeweled dagger and a gold and lapis lazuli ax, both covered with images of the pharaoh killing his enemies and with the cartouches of Ahmose.

Ahmose also constructed a group of monuments at Abydos, which was the cult center of the god Osiris. These were designed to promote the king as an aspect of the god, and also to honor the female members of his family. Osiris was one of the most important gods of Egypt, and he was associated with death and the afterlife. From the Middle Kingdom onward, the tomb of a First Dynasty pharaoh called Djer at Abydos was actually thought to be the tomb of the god Osiris himself. Consequently the site became an important center of pilgrimage, and some people from elsewhere in Egypt chose to be buried at the site. Although New Kingdom pharaohs were never buried at Abydos, Ahmose and later rulers chose to build temples there with dummy tombs attached to them.

Ahmose's buildings there included a pyramid with a temple attached to it. This was a dummy pyramid in the sense that Ahmose did not intend to be buried under it. Rather it was intended to show his worship of the god Osiris and his recognition of the importance of Abydos. Ahmose also ordered the construction of another temple at the site, which was supervised by Neferperet using mudbricks and limestone blocks from the Tura quarry. The temples were decorated with pictures of Ahmose's campaigns against the Hyksos. Recent archaeological discoveries at the site include scenes of horses and chariots, and archers shooting arrows into the air.

Not far from his own pyramid and temple, Ahmose erected a chapel in memory of his grandmother Tetisheri. A magnificent stele was found in this chapel, which describes the idea

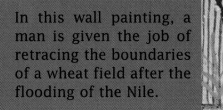

In this wall painting, a man is given the job of retracing the boundaries of a wheat field after the flooding of the Nile.

behind the building. "Now it came to pass that his majesty sat in the audience hall, the King of Upper and Lower Egypt, Nebpehtyre, Son of Ra, Ahmose, given life, while the hereditary princess, king's daughter, king's sister, great king's wife, Ahmose Nefertari, was with his majesty." After they had chatted for a while about religious rituals conducted for the souls of dead people, Ahmose Nefertari asked Ahmose what was wrong. "Why has this been remembered, why are you talking about this, what has come into your heart?" Ahmose replied that "I it is who have remembered the mother of my mother, and the mother of my father, great king's wife and king's mother Tetisheri, triumphant. She has a tomb and a memorial chapel on the soil of Thebes and Abydos. I have said this to you, in that I have desired to have made for her a pyramid and a house at Abydos as a monumental donation of my majesty." Ahmose then describes the building project to his wife, listing features including a lake, a garden, and priests to carry out rituals in honor of his grandmother. He finishes the stele by saying, "Lo, his majesty spoke this word while this was in the process of construction. His majesty did this because he so greatly loved her, beyond everything."

This stele gives us a glimpse into the relationship between Ahmose and his sister/wife, Ahmose Nefertari. It is very unusual for an Egyptian woman to be shown joining in with important decisions, and this may reveal that she was particularly interested in the religious building projects during Ahmose's reign.

DEATH OF THE KING

Ahmose died in the twenty-sixth year of his rule, 1525 BC, when he was approximately thirty-five years old. His tomb has not yet been identified, but it was probably in the cemetery at Dra Abu el-Naga in western Thebes. His body has been identified as one of those found in the tomb near Deir el-Bahri. We have no record of his burial, although he was certainly placed in a magnificent coffin and surrounded with many valuable objects and offerings. One small statue of him, in the guise of a mummy, is known. This kind of statuette was called a *shabti* figure. These were often placed in tombs from the Middle Kingdom onward. The purpose of a shabti was to take the place of the tomb owner in the afterlife, when they were expected to do unpleasant tasks. Because the afterlife was thought to be very like Egypt itself, with a river, fields, and farms, it was thought that people would have to produce their own food and drink. Shabtis could therefore come to life and do the hard work while the dead person relaxed. Some look like the dead person, and some like their servants, but their jobs would have been the same. Sometimes shabti figures have the appropriate spell or prayer carved on them in order to make them work. Shabti figures are a good example of the typical way in which the Egyptians were able to combine elaborate religious beliefs with practical solutions.

Another example of this practical approach was the system of mummification. Egyptians believed that the soul, or *ka*, of a dead person lived in his or her dead body. If for some reason the body disappeared or was not available, then the ka could live on in statues or pictures, but the body itself was thought of as the best option. Consequently, Egyptians developed an efficient way of preserving dead bodies for as long as possible, preferably forever.

During the Predynastic Period, people were buried in the desert near their settlements. Putting a body into hot, dry sand meant that it dried out rather than decayed, and many bodies

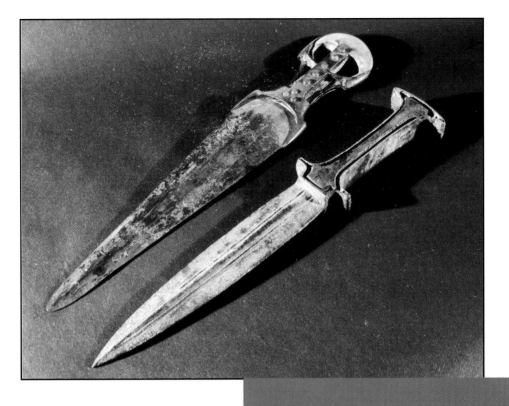

have been found with
well-preserved skin
and hair still sticking
to the bones. During the early Dynastic Period,
bodies were tightly wrapped all over in layers of
linen bandages.

Military daggers used by Egyptian soldiers

By the time of the Old Kingdom, peoples'
internal organs, including their stomachs, livers,
and intestines, were removed and buried sepa-
rately, and the bandages wrapping their bodies
were soaked in resin. When the resin dried and
hardened, it retained the shape of the body even
though the soft tissues had decomposed inside.

By the beginning of the Eighteenth Dynasty
there had been significant advances in the
processes of mummification. Along with the

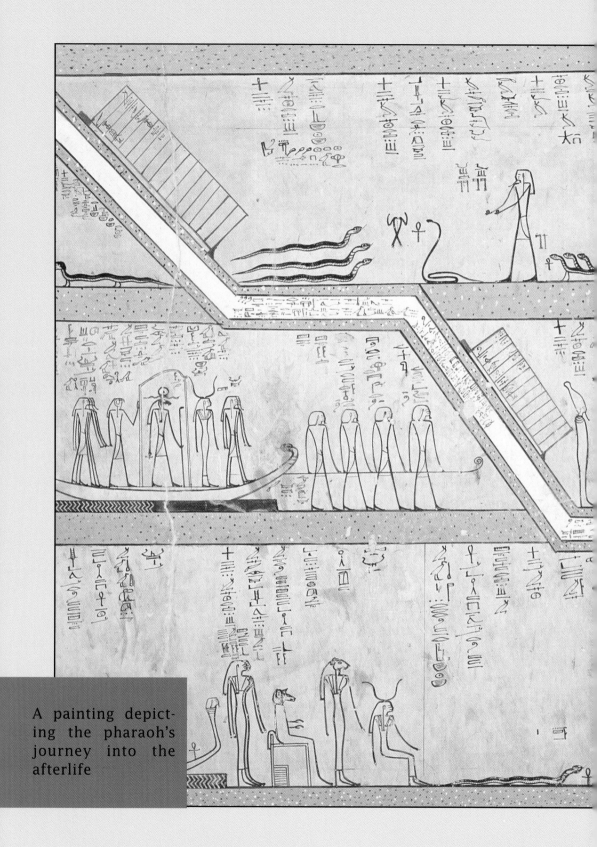

A painting depicting the pharaoh's journey into the afterlife

removal of the soft organs of the chest and abdomen, the brain was also extracted after death. The soft organs of the chest and abdomen were extracted through an incision made in the left side of the body. Brain removal was usually achieved by inserting a chisel into a nostril and pushing hard in order to break the ethmoid bone. A hook was then inserted in order to break up and drag out pieces of brain. Sometimes the body would be turned upside down and oil or vinegar would be injected into the skull through the nasal hole in order to speed up the disintegration of the brain. The stomach, intestines, lungs, and liver were preserved in natron, a naturally occurring salt found in the western desert, and placed into four canopic jars. These each had a small model of the head of the dead person as a stopper.

The emptied body would then be laid out on a bench and

covered in natron salt. The body's fluids would gradually seep into the salt, and after forty days the body would have been thoroughly dried out and would end up weighing less than one-quarter of its original weight. At this stage the body could be stuffed or padded in order to retain a lifelike impression. Linen bandages, mud, and even sand were sometimes used to replace the missing internal organs. The remodelled body was then carefully wrapped in linen bandages with magical charms and amulets placed between the layers of wrappings. The body was then finally placed into a coffin, which was sometimes put into further coffins, each one bigger than the last.

The body of Ahmose was found with a group of other royal mummies in 1871. The brain had been removed after death through a cut in the back of his neck, which was unusual. His skull was then filled with a ball of linen soaked in resin. The body of his sister/wife Ahmose Nefertari was found in the same tomb. Her internal organs had been removed through an incision in the left side of her body. This cut was then sealed with a plug of resin-soaked linen and covered with a metal plate. Ahmose Nefertari lived until old age, and evidence from her mummy shows that she suffered from hair loss. The embalmers solved this problem by giving her twenty strings of twisted human hair over her head, and attaching longer plaits to these. They also wove other plaits into her existing hair. The mummy of Queen Tetisheri also had artificial hair, and it is possible that female hair loss was a family trait.

THE AFTERMATH

Ahmose was succeeded by his son Amenhotep I, who ruled between 1525 and 1504 BC. Like his father before him, he came to the throne when he was still a boy. His mother, Ahmose Nefertari, followed the example set by both her mother, Ahhotep, and grandmother, Tetisheri, by acting as regent for the first few years of his reign. In fact, Ahmose Nefertari outlived her husband and son, and is known to have been alive during the first year of the reign of the following pharaoh, Thutmose I, who ruled from 1504 to 1492 BC. We do not know exactly when she died, but her enormous coffin, which is over ten feet long, is in the Cairo Museum.

Ahmose Nefertari's fame and importance did not end with her death. Together with her son Amenhotep I, she was worshiped through-out the New Kingdom by the occupants of the

A wall painting showing the preparation of fowl, probably ducks

village of Deir el-Medina on the West Bank at Thebes. This was the home of the builders and craftsmen who made the royal tombs in the Valley of the Kings and the memorial temples to the pharaohs on the flood plain below.

Ahmose Pennekheb and Ahmose, son of Abana, continued to serve in the army. Ahmose Pennekheb took part in the campaigns of the next four pharaohs, Amenhotep I, Thutmose I, Thutmose II, and Thutmose III, and eventually died during the joint reign of Thutmose III and Hatshepsut. His tomb autobiography lists the many campaigns that he went on and the rewards that the pharaohs had given him. He boasted that, "I followed the kings of Upper and Lower Egypt . . . I was with their majesties when they went to the South and North country, in every place where they went." His tomb autobiography ends by saying, "I have reached a good old age, having had a life full of royal favor, having had honor under their majesties and the love of me having been in the court."

Ahmose, son of Abana, took part in further campaigns in Nubia under the pharaohs Amenhotep I and Thutmose I, as well as the Syrian campaigns of Thutmose I that reached as far north as the Euphrates River. He eventually reached the rank of commander of a ship, and was rewarded with large areas of land in his home town of Elkab. His tomb records the following: "I was brave in his presence in the bad water, in the towing of the ship over the cataract. Thereupon I was made crew commander." He was a wealthy man when he died, and was able to leave his descendants well provided for. His son, Itruri, and his grandson, Paheri, both became tutors to the pharaohs' children, and Paheri became mayor of Elkab. We know that Ahmose's grandson, Paheri, was also in charge of the decoration of the tomb, and there is a small picture of Paheri standing behind his grandfather on the east wall of the tomb. The decoration seems to have been finished just before the death of Ahmose, son of Abana, and the end of his tomb autobiography reads, "I have grown old; I have reached old age. Favored as before, and loved by my lord, I rest in the tomb that I myself made."

GLOSSARY

Avaris   Capital city of the Fifteenth-Dynasty Hyksos kings in the eastern Delta, called Tell el-Daba today

cultivation or peret   The season between September and April during which crops were planted and ripened.

Deir el-Bahri   Site of the memorial temple of Hatshepsut called Djeser Djeseru, meaning Holiest of Holies.

Dra Abu el Naga   A cemetery area on the West Bank at Thebes used for burial by the rulers of the Seventeenth and early Eighteenth Dynasties before the Valley of the Kings.

dynasty   A succession of rulers from the same family or line. There were thirty-one dynasties stretching from Menes in the First Dynasty until the invasion of Alexander the Great in 332 BC. The reason for the change from one dynasty to the next is not always clear, but is usually connected to a change in the royal family or the location of the capital.

God's Wife of Amen   An important temple post based at Karnak Temple and usually filled by the wife, daughter, or mother of the pharaoh.

harvest or shemu   The season between April and June when crops were harvested.

Hyksos   A group of people from Canaan who ruled part of Egypt from Avaris during the Second Intermediate Period.

inundation or akhet   The annual flooding of Egypt, which took place between June and September.

ka   The soul in ancient Egyptian. When an individual died, the ka continued to live on. It needed feeding and looking after, which led to the development of funerary cults, where either food and drink or pictures of food and drink were offered to the ka.

Kush   A region of Nubia, also called Upper Nubia; Kush was the land between the second and fourth cataracts of the Nile, with the capital at Kerma.

Lower Egypt   The northern half of the country stretching from Memphis to the Mediterranean coast.

Maat   A goddess who embodied aspects of truth, justice, and harmony in the universe. The power of Maat regulated the seasons and the movement of the sun, the moon, and the stars. One of the main jobs of the king was to maintain the rule of Maat.

Medjay   A nomadic group from the eastern deserts of Nubia who were employed in the Egyptian army.

memorial temple A temple where the mortuary cult of the king was celebrated.

Memphis The capital city of ancient Egypt, close to modern-day Cairo. The city was known as Ineb-hedj, or White Walls, and was the cult center of the god Ptah.

nomes The forty-two districts or provinces that Egypt was divided into and which the Egyptians called sepat. These became known as nomes in the Ptolemaic period.

Nubia The region immediately south of ancient Egypt (modern Sudan).

pharaoh An Egyptian word meaning "king." In the Old Kingdom, the most common terms for the king were *hemef*, "His Majesty," or *nesw*, "King." From the New Kingdom onward the term "Pharaoh" was used, which came from the name of the palace, which was *per-aa*, or Great House.

Sile A fortress on the edge of the eastern Nile Delta marking the frontier of Egypt; the starting point of a road leading across the northern edge of the Sinai Desert.

Upper Egypt The southern half of the country stretching from Memphis to Aswan.

Valley of the Kings The New Kingdom royal necropolis located on the west bank of the Nile, about three miles west of modern-day Luxor.

vizier The chief minister of the government, also called the *tjat*. During the New Kingdom there were two viziers at Memphis and Thebes.

Wawat Also called Lower Nubia, the areas of land surrounding the river Nile between Aswan, or the first cataract of the Nile, and the second cataract.

FOR MORE INFORMATION

ORGANIZATIONS

American Research Center in Egypt
  (U.S. Office)
Emory University West Campus
1256 Briarcliff Road, NE
Building A, Suite 423W
Atlanta, GA
(404) 712-9854
e-mail: arce@emory.edu

International Association of
  Egyptologists (USA Branch)
Department of Ancient Egyptian,
  Nubian, and Far Eastern Art
Museum of Fine Arts
465 Huntington Avenue
Boston, MA 02115

JOURNALS

Ancient Egypt
Empire House
1 Newton Street
Manchester M1 1HW
England
e-mail: empire@globalnet.co.uk

WEB SITES

Due to the changing nature of Internet links, the Rosen Publishing Group, Inc., has developed an online list of Web sites related to the subject of this book. This site is updated regularly. Please use this link to access the list:

http://www.rosenlinks.com/lae/ahmo/

FOR FURTHER READING

Aldred, Cyril. *Jewels of the Pharaohs*. London: Thames & Hudson, 1971.

Aldred, Cyril. *The Egyptians*. London: Thames & Hudson, 1998.

Baines, John, and Jaromir Malek. *Atlas of Ancient Egypt*. New York: Facts on File, 1993.

Davies, Vivian, and Renee Friedman. *Egypt Uncovered*. New York: Stewart, Tabori & Chang, 1998.

Hayes, William. *The Scepter of Egypt 2: The Hyksos Period and the New Kingdom*. New York: Metropolitan Museum of Art, 1990.

O'Connor, David. *Ancient Nubia, Egypt's Rival in Africa*. Philadelphia: University of Pennsylvania Museum, 1993.

Redford, Donald. *Egypt, Canaan, and Israel in Ancient Times*. Princeton, NJ: Princeton University Press, 1992.

Robins, Gay. *Women in Ancient Egypt*. London: British Museum Press, 1993.

Shaw, Ian. *Egyptian Warfare and Weapons*. Princes Risborough, England: Shire, 1991.

Shaw, Ian, and Paul Nicholson. *British Museum Dictionary of Ancient Egypt*. London: British Museum Press, 1995.

Spencer, A. Jeffrey. *Death in Ancient Egypt*. New York: Penguin, 1991.

BIBLIOGRAPHY

Bietak, Manfred. *Avaris: The Capital of the Hyksos.* London: British Museum Press, 1996.

Breasted, James. *Ancient Records of Egypt Vol II: The Eighteenth Dynasty.* Chicago: University of Chicago Press, 2001.

Davies, Vivian, and Louise Schofield. *Egypt, the Aegean and the Levant.* London: British Museum Press, 1995.

Kemp, Barry. *Ancient Egypt: Anatomy of a Civilization.* London: Routledge, 1989.

Lichtheim, Miriam. *Ancient Egyptian Literature Volume II: The New Kingdom.* Berkeley, CA: University of California Press, 1976.

Oren, Eliezer. *The Hyksos: New Historical and Archaeological Perspectives.* Philadelphia: University of Pennsylvania Museum, 1997.

Van den Boorn, G. *Duties of the Vizier: Civil Administration in the Early New Kingdom.* New York: Kegan Paul, 1988.

INDEX

ABOUT THE AUTHOR

Susanna Thomas has a B.A. in Egyptian archaeology from University College, London, and was awarded a Ph.D. from Liverpool University in 2000. She has worked at sites all over Egypt, including in the Valley of the Kings, and runs excavations at Tell Abqa'in in the western Delta. She is particularly interested in vitreous materials and trade in the late Bronze Age. She is currently a research fellow at Liverpool University and director of the Ramesside Fortress Town Project.

CREDITS

EDITOR
Jake Goldberg

LAYOUT
Geri Giordano

SERIES DESIGN
Evelyn Horovicz